Introduction

The ideas in this book came from a group of teachers creating alternative approaches to teaching low attaining pupils – not the customary repetitive, procedural, fragmented, disjointed, simplified mathematics often given to these students. Existing research (at the end of this introduction) supported them in this venture.

The teachers came from a wide range of rural, small town and inner city comprehensive schools. They were all taking part in the Improving Attainment in Mathematics Project, which was supported by the Esmee Fairbairn Foundation. The views expressed are those of the authors and participating teachers. This book is based on ideas that the teachers used in their classrooms.

The teachers in this project believed that students needed to start secondary mathematics on a good basis. There is a public belief that these students need to 'catch-up' by rushing through earlier concepts again very quickly. This approach could, if used unwisely, lead to a diet of repeated topics and repetitive tasks. The belief in 'catch-up' is partly generated by genuine concern about students' ability to handle more advanced concepts, partly by political targets, partly by the provision to all schools of materials with which to do this task, and partly by the misinterpretation of these materials and their purpose by school managers and governors.

We know, from research, that groups of such students are often:
- given repetitive work of a kind that is very simplified;
- offered mathematics in a step-by-step way;
- focused on arithmetic in imaginary 'everyday' contexts;
- expected to memorize unconnected topics and methods;
- expected to redo, again and again, work they have done before because they may have forgotten methods.

Project teachers believed that there were better ways of helping their students become good mathematics learners than these, which may only lead to short-term, superficial, success.

The main drive for the teachers was a set of shared beliefs, some of which are given here.

Development of reasoning and thinking

All students are entitled to learn mathematics in ways that develop thinking and confidence in problem solving. Mathematics offers, as well as numeracy skills, logical reasoning, discussion and argument about abstract ideas, an arena for careful analysis, categorization and generalization.

Right to access mathematics

While many adolescents appear to have obstacles to engagement in mathematics, all students have the right to, and are capable of, full engagement with the subject. Outstanding features of mathematics that make it interesting, and that make learning easier, are the interconnections between different topics and representations, and the relationships between and within mathematical structures.

Maths as a source of self-esteem

For a variety of reasons, success in mathematics can be a source of self-esteem for students. Some students may do better in mathematics than in other subjects, particularly if literacy is also weak. The feeling that they are progressing in a high-status subject can be valuable, particularly if they failed to make progress in their previous schools. But more than this, a positive experience of mathematics can empower them mentally because their own thoughts are being valued. Self-esteem can be developed through:
- believing that students desire to learn;
- responding to, using and generating students' own questions;

- fostering awareness of learning, such as focusing the use of practice exercises on self-assessment;
- offering challenge and support instead of simplifying the work;
- enabling students to step out of their comfort zones and take risks, such as creating their own hypotheses (for some of these students, no part of a mathematics lesson is a comfort zone);
- developing 'togetherness' in classrooms when working on mathematics.

Learners' identity

Learners can see their goal as to learn, or to finish tasks or to fit in. Some cannot see how to fit in so appear to choose not to fit in. Some see silence and inactivity as safe ways to fit in. In this project the goal of teachers was to help learners have the goal to learn. Intellectual engagement would be its own reward. There would be no need to construct artificial 'real-life' contexts as motivational devices, although authentic contexts could, of course, be used mathematically where obviously appropriate and relevant for the students.

Taking account of reality

While improvement of mathematical thinking and self-esteem are appropriate goals for educationists, students also need to be achieving in ways recognized by the outside world. Final examination results are important, but students will be better prepared for these if they understand some mathematics, and feel confident to tackle unfamiliar problems, while being sure they have some fundamental tools, such as arithmetic and calculator use.

The aim is to generate *deep progress* in mathematics.

This book shows how a group of varied teachers put their ideas into practice, in many different ways, with a range of results.

What we already know:

- In 1976 Richard Skemp described how a 'relational' understanding of mathematics was much more powerful, long lasting and useful than an 'instrumental' understanding.

- In 1986 Brenda Denvir and Margaret Brown showed that learning mathematics is not a linear process, and that being immersed in one aspect of mathematics can frequently lead to unexpected learning.

- In 1987 Afzal Ahmed published the results of a project with teachers who worked with low attaining students. They found that nearly all the students were able to use sophisticated thinking skills and learned better if they were given time to make choices, to discuss and to explore mathematics.

- In 1997 researchers at King's College London found that teachers who made connections ('connectionist teachers') were more successful than those who taught in a technical or fragmented way.

- In 1997 Jo Boaler showed that students who learned mathematics through open-ended exploration and problem solving did better in tests and other types of mathematics assessment than similar students who were taught only to perform techniques and follow procedures.

- In 1999 Carol Dweck showed that learners and teachers who believed that intelligence was flexible, and the goal was to learn as much as they could, were more successful than those who believed in finishing tasks and passing tests.

- In 2003 James Hiebert and others compared mathematics teaching in seven nations. They found that, whatever the lesson, task or assessment style, teachers in the highest achieving nations tended to focus on relationships, connections and complexities within mathematics, and not reduce everything to technical performance.

Deep progress
in learning

Concept

Defining deep progress

More good can be done by helping learners develop thinking skills and understanding throughout all their mathematics lessons, than by teaching them only to perform and remember particular methods and topics. Students are prepared to learn more mathematics and work well with mathematics in later life. All students are willing and able to work hard.

The teachers in the project all had similar sets of goals and beliefs in their teaching of students who, on entry to secondary school, had achieved less than target levels in mathematics. The main drive for the teachers was the shared belief that *all students can learn mathematics* and that efforts made to help them do so were going to be worthwhile.

The aim was to generate *deep progress* in mathematics.

Deep progress means that students:
- learn more mathematics;
- get better at learning mathematics;
- feel better about themselves as mathematics students.

Sometimes the last of these follows on from the other two. Sometimes students have to feel better before they learn more; sometimes students have to redevelop good learning habits before they can move on and learn more. Ideally, students will make progress in all three aspects.

Behaviour can be altered, but it takes time, persistence and imaginative methods. Old habits have to be replaced by new ones. An approach that offers clear expectations and disrupts old expectations might be effective. Time has to be given in lessons to establishing new habits; time must be given over several weeks for them to become 'habits'.

Application

Working on deep progress means that students:

- show confidence;
- tackle complex problems;
- are prepared to try;
- ask their own questions;
- share ideas;
- have more self-esteem;
- remember the activities and the methods;
- transfer knowledge to exam-based work.

Concept

Expected improvements

It is worth spending considerable time on developing new, mathematical habits of working. This creates a basis for development of new knowledge. All students are capable of thinking mathematically.

Whatever you mean by 'mathematical thinking', the strengthening of ways of thinking and working is important in mathematics.

The list on the page opposite shows some of the ways that you might shift your teaching so that the students are expected to do more of the work. Make a start by choosing one to build into your next lesson.

Application

Things to work on include:
- choosing appropriate techniques;
- contributing examples;
- describing connections with prior knowledge;
- finding similarities or differences beyond superficial appearance;
- generalizing structure from diagrams and examples;
- identifying what can be changed;
- making something more difficult;
- making comparisons.

Concept

Strategies for improvement

All students can benefit from opportunities to use the strategies shown on the page opposite. Like most things, if they are part and parcel of regular classroom practice the students will come to expect to work in this way.

Many of these suggestions encourage the students to take responsibility throughout the learning process – from the questions being worked on, to the range of solutions being offered.

Included in the suggestions is the opportunity for students to work on unfamiliar problems – something that low attaining students are rarely given the chance to do.

Throughout the book you will find suggestions for possible tasks you might use that involve one, some or all of the strategies listed on the opposite page.

Application

Strategies to work on include:
- generating your own enquiries;
- posing your own questions;
- predicting problems;
- giving reasons;
- working on extended tasks over time;
- creating your own methods and shortcuts;
- sharing your own methods;
- using prior knowledge;
- initiating mathematical ideas;
- dealing with unfamiliar problems;
- changing your mind with new experiences.

Concept

Behaviour

Low attaining students can be so demoralized by their previous mathematics experiences that behaviour, participation, self-belief and mathematical knowledge are all legitimate foci for change.

Behaviour can be altered, but it takes time, persistence and imaginative methods. Old habits have to be replaced by new ones over time. A 'training' approach (with clear expectations and rewards) might be effective for some aspects of behaviour, but not for everything. Anything that disrupts old expectations (including expectations of the teacher's behaviour) is worth trying. Time has to be given in lessons to establishing new patterns of behaviour, and time must be given over several weeks for them to become 'habits'.

The teachers in the project worked explicitly on contradicting ambient assumptions about behaviour. Statements such as 'they can't concentrate' were taken to mean 'they don't concentrate' and 'they can't listen' as 'they don't listen'. Teachers created lessons in which 'they do concentrate' and 'they do listen'.

Application

Getting them to arrive on time

The first student to the room gets to challenge the teacher in a game.

Take it in turns to remove one, two or three counters; the person to remove the last counters wins.

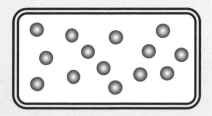

Taking full part in the lesson

Thinking – students know that anyone in the class might be asked to answer, after some thinking time.

Contributing – pairs of students discuss mathematics and all pairs have to report back on what they have found.

Listening – aural questions are used at the start of lessons, even as students come in, as a settling-down task.

Responsibility – students are given special books in which they record their chosen examples as a reminder.

Taking pride in work

Every student keeps his/her own work in a folder so that at the start of a lesson the student has something to open and start doing. The folder contains tasks and resources that trigger memory from the last lesson.

Concept

Challenge and struggle

Challenge and struggle are part of learning mathematics. All students should have the opportunity to work with a challenge. Struggle is part of this challenge and effort is required.

The teachers in the project found each student's comfort zone, then planned at times to move beyond this. Moving beyond the comfort zones should become a regular feature of classroom practice. A student's view of him/herself as a learner and specifically as a learner of mathematics can change. In the project, students became more willing to deal with difficult work through higher expectations and support.

Application

1. What are these numbers doing? How does this multiplication method work?

532×689

```
        1 2
      4 0 2 7
  3 0 2 4 1 8
    1 8 1 6
        4 5
  _____
  3 6 6 5 4 8
```

2. If you have some fraction calculators try using the addition constant to create some fraction sequences. So the sequence for adding $\frac{1}{7}$ gives:

$$\frac{1}{7}, \ \frac{2}{7}, \ \frac{3}{7}, \ \frac{4}{7}, \ \frac{5}{7}$$

However the arithmetic sequence for $\frac{1}{12}$ gives:

$$\frac{1}{12}, \ \frac{1}{6}, \ \frac{1}{4}, \ \frac{1}{3}, \ \frac{5}{12}$$

What is happening? Find other fraction arithmetic sequences that give the same list for the numerators.

Concept

Silent moments

Concentration was something that all the teachers worked on with their students. Generally students are not used to being quiet, so learning to be quiet with their own thoughts was one of the aims that the teachers in the project had for their students.

Various strategies were used to create peaceful moments throughout the various parts of the lesson – some of these are shown on the opposite page. Working silently on your own ideas before sharing with others was one of these strategies. The aim was to emphasize that thinking sometimes requires all your attention and focus and so is best done in quiet moments.

Application

- Read out answers once only, very quietly.

- Ask your students to look at a problem on the board in silence, not for them to solve it, but to think hard about, then ask them for ideas.

- Give your class the same sheet of multiplication facts to complete at the start of every lesson and work through it in silence for 15 minutes. The aim is to complete more and more each time (each student competes with their previous personal best).

- Ask a student to describe the picture below to the rest of the class. As s/he describes it ask the rest of the students to draw what they hear. No one is allowed to ask questions about meaning. This is a good activity for working on language.

Concept

Structures of lessons

The following page gives some examples of lesson structures to show the variety used by teachers working in the project. There was no uniform lesson style, although all contained some discussion and sharing (not always as a whole group), some mental work and some reflection on previous work.

Contrary to a common belief that low attaining students and 'difficult' classes need frequent changes of activity, the teachers in the project worked on developing sustained activity and opportunities for thinking about what they were doing.

Imagine the learning of a topic taking place over a period of time. The important thing is how to engage the students in their own learning.

TIP:
Try different structures for lessons – three-part lessons are not mandatory! Why not try four-part lessons or two-part lessons?

Application

Lesson A

Aural questions are used as a settling device. Students work in silence on their own, followed by discussion of answers and methods in which they mark their own work. Then comes an activity that starts with the teacher demonstrating and orchestrating discussion about possible ways to tackle tasks. Students work on a worksheet that includes being asked to make up their own questions to tackle. The 'own questions' tasks act as a reflective device; there is no final whole-class time.

Lesson B

Students continue work started in a previous lesson, writing down their findings on small whiteboards to share; they are finding 'odd ones out' from a collection of shapes, according to some constraints. After this there is discussion about what was found in previous lessons, and students can then create their own questions to continue exploring. At the end of the lesson, students share findings and use an overhead projector to show what they have found.

Lesson C

Students start with a number challenge. They volunteer to write their suggestions on the board that have been worked out mentally. About halfway through the lesson the new topic is started, for example data-handling. They brainstorm everything they recall about it. They each have to invent five questions to ask people, and the whole class discusses potential difficulties with collecting data to answer the questions. Almost the entire lesson is whole-class discussion.

Lesson D

Students are given a worksheet and materials to cut out and manipulate to find reflections without using tracing paper or mirrors. They make up two questions to be answered by their partner. They can check their work by constructing the 'same' reflections using tracing paper. There is no whole-class discussion.

Concept

Joining in with your mind

There is a connection between engagement and learning; students cannot learn unless they are engaged, and engagement is a combination of social, emotional, intellectual and task characteristics. Teachers have to work on all these facets to ensure engagement. All learners can develop their concentration and participation skills.

The page opposite shows some ways in which the teachers explicitly generated a studious atmosphere of concentration and participation. Of course this takes time, but you should not give up trying to achieve these. Remember though that participation does not always imply concentration. Learners can be involved physically, such as taking part in a physical representation of a graph or of a data set, without concentrating on meaning. However, in order to concentrate one has to participate to some extent.

The quality and patterns of interaction can be changed so that students participate in the creation of mathematics in the classroom. Gradual shifts can be made so that students are more responsible for their own learning. It is important that the students' work is valued both by the teacher and other students.

Application

- Ask students to check and make comments about each other's work.
- Get students to listen to, or read, questions in detail before they answer.
- Give students the responsibility to monitor their own efforts.
- Get everyone, including the teacher and teaching assistants, to describe how they use imagined diagrams, arm-waving, inner speech, sounds, symbols and other squiggles when thinking about maths.
- Ask students to imagine something and give time for the image to develop.
- Expect everyone to contribute.

Concept

Learning and moving

Some students find using pen and paper unhelpful for their learning. Try other ways to engage the students using verbal, visual and practical methods and activities that involve some movement.

Sorting numbers into order using the students as a number line is something that many teachers use. Doing activities like those shown on the page opposite supports participation (as everyone has a card), which is essential for concentration, but does not *guarantee* mental concentration.

How do you notice when your students are thinking?

Application

Give everyone a card with a number on it (choose the numbers for your class – integers, fractions, decimals, a mix of numbers). Here are some suggestions (there are infinite variations).

1. Put yourselves in order.

2. Stand next to someone so that you have a difference of 2 (or 3 or 4, for example). Find others to connect to each of you. Who belongs in your group?

3. Find another person so that:
   - your numbers add to 30 .
   - your numbers are greater than 20 when multiplied.

If everyone needs to be paired how would you organize the rest of the class?

4. Numbers that are factors of 60 stand on my right and numbers that are factors of 49 stand on my left.

5. Numbers that are multiples of 3 stand on my right and numbers that are multiples of 5 stand on my left.

Concept

Speaking and listening

Make 'listen to each other' important. You can achieve this by asking for students to state ideas in their own words, or to take each other's ideas into account in their answers, or to do some work based on another student's idea. This could be done implicitly; for example, one teacher asked: 'Can you say that again to Mark because you are saying it very well?'

All teachers in the project used 'hands-down thinks'. The class all sits and thinks and anyone might be asked to answer. There is extended time to think about their answer.

Application

- Ask students to explain ideas, concepts and definitions in their own words.
- Ask questions with multiple answers that everyone can answer to ensure all can participate; generate several answers for the class to consider.
- Ask students to give answers to worked questions.
- Ask students to create questions for each other.
- Ask each student to produce something to contribute to the class; this work can be compared, classified or ranked according to mathematical power. For example:

Find six ways to shade a half of these shapes.

Concept

Getting a good discussion

Tasks that need data input from everyone in the class are less intimidating than ones that require a single answer.

If everyone works on the same questions students can wait until they hear the answer, get fed up because someone has found the answer before they did, or get fed up because they got the answer wrong.

Using questions that have some variation means that all the students can find solutions. Since the answers are different and possibly unique, the students all have a reason to share and use mathematical language to tell you what they did and how they did it.

Application

1. Put two lines crossing on a page. Measure the angles. Repeat until you have an idea to share.

2. Find five numbers that have a mean of 4, a median of 3 and a mode of 2.

   How many sets of numbers are there? What is the same about these sets of numbers?

3. Using a fraction calculator, find three fractions that add to make 1 but which all have 1 as the numerator.

   Is there anything special about the denominators?

Concept

Question types

The quality and patterns of interaction can help students participate in the creation of the mathematics in the classroom. The way a teacher talks about mathematics, asks questions about it and treats students' answers will strongly influence the way students see the subject and the way they feel about their own learning of it.

What kinds of questions do you ask your students? Watson & Mason (1998) offer some ideas for thinking about question types and also different ways of asking questions in the classroom. On the right are some suggestions that may help you start to think about this issue.

Application

- Use closed questions about things that are puzzling, intriguing, interesting, unexpected, unusual; don't use closed questions to 'catch them out'.
- Use open questions to explore possibilities, or to gather raw material; don't use them just to get people to speak.
- Use questions to expose an argument; get students to say the argument in their own words to each other.
- Get learners to use technical language out loud. Make it a game, have a chorus!
- Gather what everyone says onto the board for sorting, organizing, erasing, and discussing at a later stage.

Concept

Using learners' responses

It is possible for teachers to undo past negative experiences and attitudes by finding ways to use learners' responses as a positive contribution to lessons.

Different kinds of questions produce different kinds of participation. It is important for teachers to use different types of questions to encourage the students to take part in the lesson.

The teachers in the project had a range of standard questions they used frequently enough so that the students began to expect them and could even begin to ask some of them themselves. The page opposite shows some of the questions that were asked. Ask students to give answers and methods or reasons and invite them to comment on each other's answers. Extended waiting time is used both before and after the answers are given. Encourage the use of technical language.

Application

What is the same and what is different about … ?

Give me an example of … .

Give me a … which is not a … .

Is it always, sometimes or never true that … ?

Why … ?

Concept

Creating discussion between students

By the time they get to secondary school, many students are out of the habit of discussing ideas with each other in mathematics lessons. It is possible, with persistence, consistence and insistence, to re-establish this habit.

Most adolescents will eventually respond well to high expectations, and to having the opportunity to discuss. Just as teachers at a meeting or conference will sometimes be found discussing things other than the task in hand, so will adolescents. Over-control of discussion will restrict useful, spontaneous discussion about mathematics as well as 'off task' topics.

Application

Ordering

Put the algebraic expressions in order of size for $x = 3$

$$x + 2 \qquad 2x \qquad 3x - 1 \qquad x - 2 \qquad x \qquad 1 - x$$

Use other values of x to reorder the expressions. Which values of x change the order of the expressions and which values of x keep the expressions in the same order?

(Vary the task by changing the expressions.)

Matching

1. Match histograms to box and whisker diagrams.

2. Match some co-ordinate pairs to some lines.

3. Use a set of loop dominoes with fractions and decimals to play matching the cards.

Concept

Working in pairs

Peaceful social interaction takes time to establish. Mutual respect in mathematical discussion can be used effectively where the teacher is not the focus of all the remarks. Gradual shifts can be made towards students being more responsible for their own learning.

On the right are some activities that the students might work on in pairs. Give them time to discuss and share ideas. Ask everyone to make notes on what they have found before the whole class comes together for a discussion.

TIP:
Before you expect an answer give students time to think.

THINK   PAIR   SHARE

Application

Sorting

1. Sort some triangles (or quadrilaterals) using a particular property such as those that are isosceles and those that are not isosceles. (Knowing that something does NOT belong to a set is useful knowledge.)

2. Sort some graphs, which are plotted on different scaled axes, according to their gradients.

Arguing about conflicting situations

1. $\dfrac{1}{1} = 1 \qquad \dfrac{2}{2} = 1 \qquad \dfrac{3}{3} = 1 \qquad$ so $\dfrac{0}{0} = ?$

2. 0.9999999... equals 1, or does it?

Reacting to answers

3

Concept

Shifting responsibility to students

The way a teacher reacts to answers has an emotional, social and mathematical effect on lessons. You can choose whether to react to all answers, to right answers, to wrong answers or to no answers. Sometimes no reaction promotes thought; sometimes an enthusiastic reaction promotes a good feeling about achievement.

A teacher should listen to responses and use them to decide where the lesson should go next. Is it time to move on, to recapitulate, to provide more rehearsal space? The less articulate the learners, the more agile the teacher needs to be.

TIP:
Don't be the only 'place' where students ask about answers.

Application

- Ask a question and then give students time to plan their answers with a friend.
- What if no one answers? Knowing that you don't know is OK. Get someone to ask the question again but in their own words.
- Checking your own answers is a good idea – here are some suggestions:

  - When you have solved equations, check by substitution.

  - When you have divided, use a calculator to multiply.

  - When you have calculated a missing angle, use it to recalculate one you were given.

  - If you input numbers systematically, do the outputs also have some kind of pattern?

$105 \div 7 = 15$

Concept

Focusing on questioning answers

One of the aims all teachers should have is to make their students bold enough to give answers to questions. The teacher can then decide how to respond to these. Students can shift towards reflecting on answers if the goal of the lesson is changed slightly. Try to pose questions that will produce answers that are useful to the lesson, and that everyone will listen to. This could be achieved by asking the students to:

- find three facts, ideas, methods that were new to them this lesson;
- pick out the hardest question they tackled and make up one that is as hard;
- construct an example that they could show to a younger student to explain what they had been doing.

How can teachers focus on questioning answers rather than answering questions? To establish this way of working it must become habitual.

Application

- Put a range of answers on the board; discuss why they are right or wrong. (Display anonymous mini-whiteboards.)
- Do not respond immediately to answers but wait – hold the silence and see what happens.
- Ask how incorrect answers are arrived at; ask about correct answers too. Discuss which methods work only for this example, and which would work for other cases.
- Ask students to discuss what needs to be said to mythical learners who produce typical 'wrong answers'.

What has gone wrong here? Ask students to plan what they would say to help this learner find the correct answer.

$$943$$
$$684 \; -$$
$$\overline{341}$$

Concept

Dealing with unexpected answers

If you have taken steps to shift responsibility to learners, you have also made it more likely that answers and ideas that may derail your plans will emerge.

Sometimes there are answers that you were not expecting, which you don't understand, which are wrong and worrying, or which open up pathways that reveal some lack in your planning. The possibility of these is what often hinders teachers being more open to discussion in their classrooms.

TIP:
It is important to listen for direction-changing answers.

Application

- If you cannot make sense of a student's method, ask them to make up a new question that is similar and work through it together.
- Ask if anyone else can explain it.
- Thank students for unexpected answers, saying 'I had no idea that anyone would be thinking like that – thank you very much, I've learned something'.
- Ask, 'Can anyone find an example where this doesn't work?'

Concept

Storing good ideas

One way of dealing with a range of different responses to an activity is to share good ideas on a wall poster. All responses can then be acknowledged and validated, which will encourage students to give more ideas. These can be used later in the lesson for a discussion or possibly to start another lesson or within another lesson.

Writing for the wall encourages not only that the results/ideas about the mathematics are to be shared but, since the findings are public, the reasoning and possible proof for the finding/ideas have to be clearly and explicitly written by the student.

TIP:
You can also use this idea for an unexpected response in a lesson.

Application

Store good ideas on a wall poster for later (for example,
'Who wants to find examples of this for homework?').

Marie's Idea

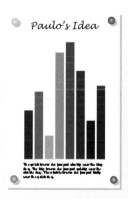

Paulo's Idea

Giving time

4

Concept

Immersion in a topic world

Extended time for exploring a topic means that every student has had time to understand something new. It can take a long time, and several experiences, for learners to reach the goal the teacher has for them. It can take a long time to connect new experiences to past experiences. The learning that takes place on these journeys may be dense and busy, but hard to identify in terms of curriculum topics or other people's goals.

Think about discussing this with students explicitly. Enrol teaching assistants in these ideas of slow discovery.

Application

Help learners understand that learning is not a straightforward, linear journey.

Help learners recognize when they have grasped an important mathematical idea.

Help learners understand how the work they have done, and the efforts they have made, have contributed to their long-term learning.

Some teachers use a small area of mathematics, but work it over and over for a few weeks using several representations, different language forms, varied types of questions and students' own ideas, so that in the end students:

- know the topic very well;
- know how it relates to other topics;
- know how to make mathematically powerful choices;
- feel very confident about a key area of mathematics;
- feel very confident about working with mathematical ideas;
- can make suggestions, take risks and evaluate their own progress.

Concept

Deep connections

Take a topic and think about it in a range of ways and contexts – resources, movement and writing, speaking and listening. Search for different ways for the students to work on this mathematics. Connect it to other topics that the students have met or will meet. See how far you can develop this over a period of time.

The opposite page shows one example of the ideas a teacher used for an activity focused on difference (developed from a sequence of lessons). As well as arithmetic related to difference and constructing representations, the students considered negative numbers and algebraic symbols.

Application

- Discuss 'difference' and 'subtraction', and get students to show, on a number line, pairs of numbers that give a difference of two.
- Use strips of paper, rods or cubes, two units long, and place them anywhere on the line. Discuss the end points, not always integers.
- Use counting on, counting back, 'distance between'.
- Move beyond small whole positive numbers to negatives, decimals, pairs of numbers that bridge zero, or bridge tens. Have two-unit strips that have given end points. Ask students to find where to put them.
- Sort pairs of numbers according to the size of their differences; make up pairs.
- Label the strips so that they can be used for *any* suitable end points. For example, a strip $1\frac{1}{2}$ units long can be labelled in many ways, including: $(x + 1\frac{1}{2}) - x$ or $y - (y - 1\frac{1}{2})$
- Discuss the everyday language of difference (distance between places, drops and rises in temperature and so on).
- Can difference be negative?
- Represent number as: lines; grids; whole numbers; decimal numbers; vertical and other scales.
- If you call the hidden number m, you are looking for $m + 2$ or $m - 2$.

Concept

Thinking is more important than finishing

Students can only make deep progress at an individual pace, not at an externally imposed rhythm that may be based on 'doing' techniques, rather than learning concepts. The problem for teachers is how to help them improve their pace, and the quality of their learning, while recognizing that understanding mathematical ideas takes time. This is such a hard issue for teachers under curriculum pressure that it is tempting to focus on coverage, and this leads to an emphasis on 'doing and finishing' rather than 'thinking and learning'.

Successful teachers provide structures that allow different times to think, emphasize and reward thinking, and provide targets that allow learners to feel mathematical progress.

Application

Doing exercises

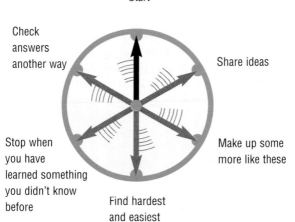

Start

Check answers another way

Share ideas

Make up some more like these

Stop when you have learned something you didn't know before

Find hardest and easiest

Answering questions

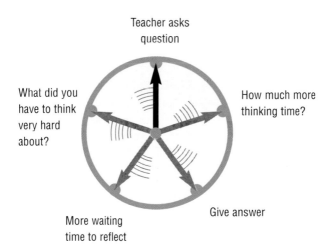

Teacher asks question

What did you have to think very hard about?

How much more thinking time?

More waiting time to reflect

Give answer

Concept

I got rhythm...

The contrast between working quickly and fluently and working slowly and thoughtfully can be discussed with students, so they can see there are different ways to learn different aspects of mathematics. 'Own pace' can be slowed down by disengagement, but here the focus is on engagement so that working slowly does not equate with 'wasting time'. However, there are times when working quickly is important:

- to establish automatic responses;
- to get a sense of pattern;
- to get initial stages of some work ready to use as tools for future work;
- to generate enough data for patterns to be appreciated.

Application

1. Chant tables or procedures repeatedly until words become automatic.

2. Use rhythm to appreciate pattern, for example:
   - counting up in fives
   - counting up in 0.1 or $\frac{1}{10}$
   - counting down from 101 in steps of 1.1 or $1\frac{1}{10}$

3. Emphasize structure orally – for example, get the students to say this:

   Two times all of $a + b$ is *two* times a and *two* times b.

   Three times all of $a + b$ is *three* times a and *three* times b (and so on).

Concept

Working quickly and reflecting slowly

Use a rapid thought-splurge to tackle an unfamiliar problem – generate lots of ideas before deciding where to start. Write up every idea – the variation is revealing in terms of how the students see and connect their knowledge of mathematics.

After getting lots of ideas on the board, review them to decide which of them would be a good starting place. Possibly get the students, in pairs, to consider the different answers to work out what they think might be useful for finding the solution to the problem and what they would definitely reject.

Application

1. In deciding which properties to use to sort out a group of shapes the students might call out 'parallel lines', 'angles of a triangle', 'acute and obtuse angles' and 'right angles'. These are written quickly on the board. Then take time to decide which to use.

2. Making a quick guess at the value of an unknown angle p before calculating will give an indication of the students' understanding of angles.

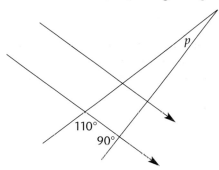

3. Quickly work out the answers to these:

$$7 \times \tfrac{1}{7} \qquad 14 \times \tfrac{1}{7} \qquad 21 \times \tfrac{1}{7} \qquad 28 \times \tfrac{1}{7} \qquad 35 \times \tfrac{1}{7}$$

Then use them as data for slow reflection. Make up another set like this one. Continue any patterns you see.

Concept

Extending tasks

Try working to sustain students' interest in a topic over time, not varying the task and topic frequently, but encouraging deeper thought in a variety of ways.

Sustaining work on one topic over a period of time promotes deep progress, awareness of progress and hence self-esteem and a sense of being a learner of mathematics. Concentration and participation enable tasks to be extended, through learners being actively engaged in thought. The relationship between these aspects is complex and non-linear; one does not guarantee another. There is no such thing as 'a guaranteed extendable task'. The extension is created by the class, the task, the teacher and the learning.

Some of the ways this can be achieved are:

- When a student has 'finished', the teacher shows how further questions can be posed about the same problem situation.
- Teachers ask 'Why?' and 'What if?' to encourage reasoning and justification, or further exploration of changes of different variables. This also models the kinds of deep questioning that students can do for themselves in future.
- All hypotheses are followed with 'Why?'.
- Giving something familiar, in an unfamiliar form, helps make connections as well as doing the task.
- Offering repetition for familiarity, but with significant variations each time, achieves fluency through accumulated experiences and gives students a sense of the range of possibilities in a topic.
- The opportunity for students to make a personal toolkit for a topic, so that opening the toolkit at the start of each lesson triggers the memory for what was done before, also provides raw material for new questions.
- A situation in which there are various mathematical objects or examples produced, or statements such as facts or conjectures, provide opportunity to work on reasoning and higher levels of abstraction.

Application

- Ask students to make up their own scalars for enlargement activities. Then ask them to explore what would happen if they used negative scalars.
- Having found out that when two lines cross you get two pairs of equal angles, which are supplementary, give students a third line and ask them to find out about the angles you get if two of the lines are parallel.
- Give students a hundred square, but in a different layout (a 'snake' shape, with 100 in the top left-hand corner and 0 in the bottom right-hand corner). The teacher's aim is to use students' sense of comfort from using the familiar hundred square to think afresh about number relationships.
- Ask students to complete some work on ratios of two quantities successfully. Then offer similar work (demonstrations, practical tasks, exercises) on ratios of three quantities. This will help them become more fluent with two, and also gain more understanding about ratio. Some may want to go on to work with ratios of four quantities.
- Ask students to compile their own list of useful percentages and how to work them out. By looking at the list, students will develop their own 'harder' questions.

Concept

Structuring teaching to help memory

Memory is often a stumbling block for low attaining students. Sometimes this is because they have had a patchy school experience, so it is important that the lessons they do attend give them the opportunity to learn how to remember mathematics and how to bring it to the forefront of their minds when necessary.

If mathematics makes sense it is easier to remember. If lessons follow on, offering a meaningful development of the subject, mathematics makes more sense than if it is cut into small, disconnected chunks.

Memory for what is important needs explicit work; this includes a frequent return to main ideas, so that memory is necessary and important. Students need to know what is worth remembering. Explicit work is needed on words, techniques, facts and images to help conceptual recall.

Application

Link new topics to previous topics. For example:

- Express angle calculations in algebraic notation – even if you don't expect students to use it.
- Do fractions, ratios, percentages together so different viewpoints can be used for the same situation.
- Talk about estimates whenever you do measurements.
- Use graphs to represent data whenever possible, even if you don't expect students to do so.

At the end of the lesson, as well as the start, talk about how the topic fitted in with the previous lesson.

Put a task relating to the previous lesson on the board for silent consideration at the start of every lesson.

Ask 'what is the same and what is different?' about confusing words. For example: area and perimeter; mode, median and mean; factor and multiple; polygon and pentagon.

Have a toolkit of language, definitions and techniques to remember, ready for a new task.

Use writing, talking and diagrams to string ideas together and hence make them easier to recall.

Exercise short-term memory. For example, filling in missing digits in vertical multidigit addition requires several things to be held in the mind.

Concept

Explicit work

Learners do not know what is worth remembering. They need to be taught what is most valuable. Explicit work is needed on using words, techniques, facts and images to help conceptual recall. But overloading struggling students with meaningless mnemonics is not helpful either.

- Remembering from lesson to lesson provides continuity and inclusion.
- Deep understanding helps long-term memory.
- Remembering mathematics helps learners feel that they know something; hence self-esteem can be enhanced.
- Memory can be used to mark personal progress.

For most students, memory can develop if there is some self-esteem to be gained by doing so.

Application

■ Ask students to draw something to illustrate new words. In the next lesson give back their drawings for them to label with the new word.

■ Make cards to match examples with words.

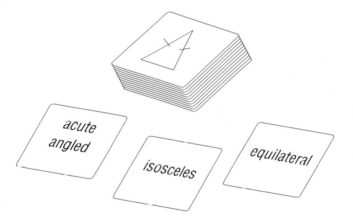

■ Repeat words, images, experiences.
■ Use concept maps or spider diagrams.
■ Ask students to make up their own ways to remember things; use these frequently and explicitly in class.
■ Tell them what the next lesson will be about and what they need to remember for it.

Concept

Doing the whole thing in your head

With frequent practice all children can become capable of multistage mental arithmetic. The challenge is to hold it all in your mind.

You can build this slowly over time with your students. Practise doing one-stage problems first – number bonds to 10, number bonds to 100, single digit times tables. Encourage them to 'beat' the calculator.

When the students are fluent add in two-stage problems with a mix of operations. Doubling and adding 3 creates shifts from even to odd numbers; multiplying by 3 and halving will lead to fractions; finding ten per cent of a number will practise aspects of place value.

On the right are some possibilities. Be demanding. For example, when asking students to calculate 52×23 it is possible for them to have a go and be successful.

Application

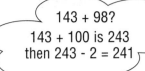

143 + 98?
143 + 100 is 243
then 243 - 2 = 241

265 + 58?
260 + 50
then add 8 + 5

So, 52 × 23 is ... ?

50 × 3 = 150
2 × 3 = 6
52 × 3 = 156

50 × 20 = 1000
2 × 20 = 40
52 × 20 = 1040

Concept

Using physical and visual memory

Learners can be reminded about past experience through a variety of senses, combining action, sound and touch.

Memory for what is important needs explicit work; this includes frequent return to main ideas so that memory is necessary and important.

Objects used for teaching – fraction charts, string for circles, help with remembering the lesson ('Do you remember when we used…') – should be introduced frequently during work on a topic so that handling the equipment brings back the memory of what it was used for.

Having given diagrams and solutions on the board, wipe them out for the students to re-create from memory – warn them that you will be doing this and help them to work on rehearsing the mathematics. Give them time to remember by reading and/or writing and ask them to rehearse the mathematics.

Ask them how they remembered something.

Application

- Use objects and equipment frequently during a topic so that handling them triggers memory.
- Return to a significant posture, or a place in the classroom, to remind students about earlier activity.
- Ask students to reconstruct an important diagram with closed eyes.
- Remove a poster from the wall and ask them what it said.

Concept

Combining words, symbols and actions

Using all the senses for teaching enhances the learning for the students.

For example, the movement generated by giving everyone a number and asking them to get into order or giving out co-ordinates and asking students to move onto a grid creates a hook for the lesson and a prompt to recall the mathematics in another lesson. Saying numbers and then clapping every three gives emphasis to the idea of multiples of three. Standing up and turning for angles or for bearings gives emphasis to the idea of turn and hence angle before representing the static picture of an angle on the board.

The suggestions opposite highlight the importance of emphasis between symbols and words and actions. When you write something, say it and point to it. Think about the order of your actions at the board.

If you work on memory over a few lessons don't forget to ask the students what they remember!

TIP:
Always leave any written information about the mathematics on the board. As you say the mathematics, show the mathematics so that the students can see and hear and read. Use all the senses to help with remembering the mathematics.

Application

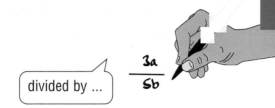

divided by ...

$$\frac{3a}{5b}$$

all multiplied by 3

$3(p+q)$

angle

imagine walking round a pentagon

Concept

Developing imagination

Students can use a range of senses to engage with, understand and remember mathematics. Teachers can ask students to imagine visual experiences, both those they have had in the past and totally imaginary ones. Slight variations in what is imagined can lead to significant differences in mathematics.

On the right are two suggestions for doing some mathematics where the students have to use their imagination. Pause after each of the statements to allow the students to adjust what they are imagining with each new, additional instruction. When the list of instructions is complete ask the students to write down what they are seeing before they discuss it with each other.

Students can use a range of senses to engage with, understand and remember mathematics. Ask students to imagine visual, tactile and physical experiences, both recalled and totally imaginary. The relationship between writing, thinking, learning and remembering is neither obvious nor trivial, especially for students who may have difficulties with general literacy.

Application

Here are two examples of some 'imagining' exercises. Ask the students to close their eyes and as you read out each line of the imagining task, pause to let them create their pictures in their heads.

1.

- Imagine a point on a circle.
- Run the point round the circle, both ways.
- Hold the point still somewhere.
- Draw an imaginary line from the point through the centre of the circle and imagine where it will meet the circle again.
- Move the point again; where does the line move?

2.

- Imagine a rectangle.
- Join the opposite corners with a line.
- Cut along the line.
- Move one of the pieces so that equal sides match.
- Describe your new shape

Concept

Using equipment

If students have something to do, physically, they can then imagine the abstract generalizations without having to go through written symbols – an obstacle for many.

Use equipment to model abstract ideas and to provide physical models. Make shapes for volume and surface area, use strips for angles and use cubes for fractions and proportion. There are many aids to calculation that represent number structure: number lines, hundred squares, base ten apparatus, Cuisenaire rods. When removing the props, it helps to ask students to imagine the familiar equipment explicitly rather than moving directly to symbolic representations.

Recognize that mathematical equipment is sometimes hard to use correctly. For example, the protractor offers lots of challenges, especially for measuring angles inside polygons. Give students lots of practice. They often forget how to use a protractor but holding one, turning it around and imagining how to use it before actual use can help to make sense of it.

Application

- Use multilink towers to represent data and discuss how to find modes, medians and means (which might be found by equalizing the towers).
- Use multilink for loci. For example, position two cubes on the desk and place other cubes so that they are equidistant from the two original cubes. Position the first two cubes in a different place and repeat.
- Use two intersecting circles of different colours to work on fractions, percentage, proportion and angle. (Take two cut-out circles, cut each on a radius and join them together.)
- Two straws crossing can create angles to be measured. Three straws help with triangles, external angles and parallel lines.
- Invent props: use a paper bag to contain an imaginary unknown number x and add and subtract numbers to it to generate expressions such as $x + 2$, $x - 3$, as well as more complicated expressions. Imagine using two bags – can you make equations to connect their quantities? More about this approach can be found in Prestage and Perks (2005).

Concept

Writing helps learning

Teachers can consider the role of writing and weigh the obstacles against the benefits, providing support, frames and scribing where this allows students to focus more on mathematics. The effort of deciding what to write about mathematics can scaffold and support the development of conceptual understanding and reasoning. It can also support students' certainty about concepts, and their memory for chains of reasoning.

Think about the use of writing and the expectations of your students.

Writing may be a particular problem for low attaining students. At the same time it is important to remember that writing offers a valuable means of communication in mathematics.

Application

- Use writing frames so that students fill in blank spaces rather than have to write arguments in full. For example: 'When I looked back over my answers I saw that these were similar ... and these were different ...'.
- Encourage students to make their own notes about what they notice or what they would like to investigate next, limiting the copying of teachers' words. For example, ask students to write down their own definition of 'difference'.
- Write students' ideas on the board in their own words. These can be hypotheses about concepts and tasks, calculations, student-generated definitions, and so on. Similarities and differences can then be discussed. For example, the teacher writes on the board the students' different definitions of 'ratio' followed by a discussion about similarities and differences.
- Allow students with severe literacy issues to communicate in other written ways. For example, when asked for a story of what $4d + 3$ could mean, allow students to draw their story while emphasizing that the objective is mathematical communication.
- Ask teaching assistants to write down exactly what students say, then read it back and ask if they want to make any changes.

Concept

Writing hinders learning

Think carefully about the purpose of the use of writing in particular instances and ask whether writing would hinder or aid learning. Writing can sometimes be a barrier to learning mathematics for students with low literacy skills. Producing written work solely to satisfy external audiences such as parents and inspectors should be avoided. Copying the teacher's words from the board or writing out the questions before answering are not useful activities as often the attention to this writing has little to do with learning mathematics.

Application

1. Symbols, for example:
'What is the value of a triangle?'

2. Spatial representations, for example:

'What is the same and what is different about these?'

3. Colour coding, for example:

$$3 \times 2 + 3 \times 5 + 3 \times 1 = 3(2 + 5 + 1)$$

Making choices

Concept

Thinking about choice

Giving choice to students means that they get involved. If you have to make a choice you have to make a decision, you cannot remain passive.

When you next plan a lesson, ask yourself how many choices are you giving to the students? Asking this question is a 'simple' way of monitoring the involvement in the lesson and in the learning that students are being given. Many of their questions create dependence. Which do you need to answer and which can you allow them to decide?

TIP:
Next time you are asked a question pause and then decide whether or not to answer it.

Application

What is the title?

Shall I use a pencil?

How big shall I make this axis?

Is this right?

Do I multiply these numbers?

What shall I do next?

How shall I write my answer?

Concept

Choosing what to do

Allowing students to choose which work to do next allows individual differentiation with students working at their own level of proximal development and at their own pace. Students can experience less stress and learn more effectively as a result. We know from experience that students tend *not* to choose easy work.

Application

- Choose a starting example for a mathematical task, such as: 'Draw your own quadrilateral, any four-sided shape you like; now join the mid-points of its sides', or 'Imagine you are cleaning the windows of a skyscraper, choose which floor you are on, now go up two floors, down five and so on'.
- Choose how hard to 'push' an idea, or extend a variable, to see what is possible. For example, 'Use the biggest and smallest number you can think of', or 'Use the most complicated number you can think of'.
- Plan lessons so that students can do 'this' or 'that'; do not give them the choice to do 'this' or 'nothing'.
- Get students involved in the planning of lessons and allow them to choose whether to spend further time on a task.

Choosing how to do it

Giving choice allows students to become emotionally attached to their work and develop their own ideas. By giving choice students can be expected to take responsibility and self-direction, whatever their attainment.

Students can be asked to account for the choices they make, thus encouraging reasoning, explanation and justification and ensuring that choices are made with mathematical understanding.

Choosing what to do gives students a sense of actively participating in their own learning. It is also harder to rebel when you have a choice of options.

Application

Choose a way of working

● plain paper	● scissors	● straws
● dotty paper	● pencils	● protractors
● pipe cleaners	● dynamic geometry software	● mini-whiteboards

Choose a method of calculation

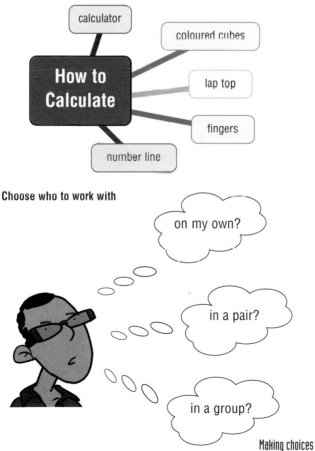

calculator

coloured cubes

How to Calculate

lap top

fingers

number line

Choose who to work with

on my own?

in a pair?

in a group?

Concept

Choosing what to do next

Being able to approach a mathematical problem in different ways is one of the enjoyments of working mathematically. Becoming aware of a variety of methods enriches learning and allows connections to be made.

It is possible to define tasks so that everyone does the same task to start with and then the students can be shown how to vary some aspect of the given task to create a new task to practise the mathematics. Some ideas are given on the right. The ambition, of course, is always for lots of work – choosing to do nothing is not an option!

Application

- Get students to choose how many examples to do in order to feel confident. Get students to choose their own examples to practise techniques.
- Get students to decide what they want to investigate about a given situation. For example, after discussing results obtained through exploring possible perimeters of shapes made by abutting four congruent squares, students can pose their own questions to explore further questions about squares and perimeters.
- Ask students to find as many different percentages of a given amount as they feel able to do after having worked on percentages.
- Get students to choose their own variation of a task within some mathematical constraints. For example, students can create their own shapes for working with transformations with vertices on the 'dots' of dotty squared paper. Then get them to do the same task but with one vertex not on a dot, two vertices not on dots and so on.

Concept

Knowing what you have learned

Students in lower sets often find it hard to know when they are making progress in mathematics. The teacher does not have to be the audience for assessment. Self-awareness is very important to their self-esteem.

There are a variety of ways in which this can be established in mathematics lessons, from the casual to the more formal. Students can get an implicit sense of their progress, and hence develop self-esteem, if tasks are structured to include a sense of progress at various stages.

A wide range of assessment activities, including self-assessment tasks, traditional testing, and so on can help students become aware of their progress. Using the ideas opposite will enable learners to sense that they are making progress throughout their work because of the way the task is structured. Students are thus in a better position to identify their own new learning.

Application

- Ask students to write their ideas on sticky labels and to stick these on a poster. Refer to them in later lessons as they explore.
- Record all ideas on the board.
- Ask students to write down their own definitions, methods, reminders when they think they have reached an understanding of something.
- Use games-type approaches to mathematics that have inbuilt mechanisms for self-monitoring progress.
- At the start of a topic give students a relatively hard task. For example, ask them to explore how 3, then 4, then 10, then 1,000 squares can be arranged to give the maximum perimeter. Ask afterwards 'Which of these tasks took you longest? Why?'. Students will find that, after a few lessons, they can do it effectively.
- Ask students to make up their own hard examples, or to 'make up one they could do now, but could not have done a week ago'.
- Give students a pre-test at the start of a topic so that what they already know can be valued and used. Let them refer frequently to their own pre-test scripts.
- Set the homework task 'Give three examples of what you have learned today' and be explicit. This is for students to reflect on their learning after the lesson and outside the mathematics classroom.

Connections and complexity

Concept

What is changing; what is staying the same?

Mathematics is a well connected body of knowledge but often students see mathematics as discrete and ill connected parts learned from one lesson to the next. Help them to work on making connections and be explicit about how each lesson follows on. Help them also to notice similarities and differences in mathematics, both between lessons and in lessons.

Don't expect students to know what is worth noticing. Be explicit about features, ways of thinking and relationships, things a stronger student might notice automatically.

Help them make connections in their work and in ways of working; help them to discern subtle differences and features of mathematics.

Application

1. Changing expressions (pay attention to the changes).

$$(x + 2)$$

$$2(x + 2) \quad (x + 3) \quad 2x + 2$$

$$3(x + 2) \quad (x + 4) \quad 3x + 2$$

2. Changing the variables and the format.

$$y = x + 2 \quad w = v + 2 \quad p = t + 2$$
$$b = 2 + c \quad f + 2 = h$$

3. Dimensions and orientation of shapes.

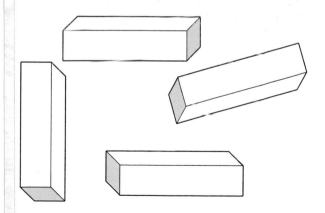

Concept

Between tasks

Sometimes a move to a new topic can be overwhelming.

Help the students to connect areas of the curriculum so that they gain a sense of security by attaching what they already know to something they are uncertain about.

As well as making the connections between the maths, explicit ways of working can also be copied. Ask 'How did you get out of a similar situation before?' when students find themselves stuck, thus indicating they could make links based on similarities in the situations. Work on their resourcefulness by modelling how to deal with being stuck.

Application

- Make explicit connections to natural numbers when multiplying positive and negative integers.
- Ask students to make their own distinctions between mathematical objects that seem superficially similar, such as:
  - means, medians and modes
  - bar charts and histograms
  - expressions and equations
  - equalities and inequalities.
- Point out things that are fundamentally the same that look different.

    1. number formats $\frac{1}{2}$ 0.5   50% $\frac{3}{6}$ 0.50000

    2. language and symbols
    - the three-times table
    - multiples of 3
    - input $\rightarrow$ ×3 $\rightarrow$ output
    - $x \rightarrow 3x$
    - $y = 3x$

    3. prisms

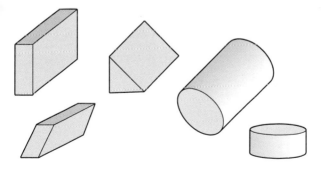

Concept

Really doing mathematics

Students can learn rigorous mathematics if the relevant kinds of rigour are discussed explicitly. Students can learn complex mathematics if there is discussion and other forms of verbalization to help them sort out the complexity. Teachers can help student learn mathematics, with all its complexities, and do not need to simplify mathematics for students, nor fudge difficult issues. Taking the complexity out of mathematics is like taking the mathematics out of mathematics.

Mathematics is beautiful in its complexity. Really doing mathematics includes this through generalizing, understanding concepts, properties and mathematical relationships. Really doing mathematics does not really require a 'real life' context.

Application

Stay with a topic long enough for deep learning and thinking to take place and restrict the need of recall.

For students to learn about angle properties, spread over time a series of shorter tasks on angles in triangles, quadrilaterals, pentagons, hexagons and angle properties of parallel lines. In these lessons, students might learn about definitions, properties and calculation techniques. Connections might be illustrated.

Remembering happens through recall.

Or

For students to learn about angle, students can be given the expanded task to explore through observation and discussion on what happens to the angles when lines cross, or not cross.

For this, give students sticks or straws. At first students are offered one stick, then two sticks, then three sticks, then as many as they like. Ask them to note what they observe, to trial and test their conjectures, to construct their own definitions. In these lessons, students learn the same things as in the lessons above and they also find out about mathematical relationships and practise general reasoning, mathematical justification and proof.

Remembering happens through reasoning and thinking.

Sorting out complexity

If something needs to be sorted then there is the potential for learning.

As well as offering ways to deal with complexity in mathematics, each of the following tactics is also an example of learning to think in appropriate ways for mathematics.

1. Discussing similarities and differences between mathematical objects and examples, thus modelling the processes of classifying that help students to make sense of variety in mathematics.

2. Tackling typical points of confusion head on, such as area and perimeter, with exploration of shapes that increase area while reducing perimeter, and vice versa.

Application

■ **True or false?** When you multiply by ten you always get a bigger answer. When you divide by ten you always get a smaller answer?

■ Explore shapes that increase in area while reducing the perimeter or increase in perimeter while reducing area.

■ Which of these work always, sometimes, never? Try different numbers.

$$25 \times 5 = 5 \times 25 \qquad 25 + 5 = 5 + 25$$

$$25 \div 5 = 5 \div 25 \qquad 25 - 5 = 5 - 25$$

Concept

Doing your own mathematics

One ambition for your students is for them to be bold enough to work on their own mathematics. Making choices about what to work on, knowing how to start, knowing what mathematics to choose, knowing what strategies to choose and knowing how to present your answers – all of these are what being a mathematician is about. Of course such activity is very different from practising finding answers ready for a test – but ultimately practising making your own decisions in this way helps the student be bolder in test situations.

TIP:
Possible questions might have already been stored from another lesson; you could give them a problem to work on to which you do not know the answer.

Application

- Show them something you have been working on; show what you have tried, and where and why you are stuck.
- Work on a problem with the students – one that you have not already worked on.
- Everyone chooses a stored question (see Storing good ideas p42) to work on quietly for a while.

Concept

A complex task

Working in the ways offered in this book requires some different thinking about teaching and often in ways that contradict normal practices and expectations. Covering content in this way might not lead to an easily observed list of topics.

The page opposite shows a task that brings together many of the elements of this book. This particular one involves homework that is needed in order to start the next lesson. It involves reasoning, making choices and recording ideas. There are links with other topics and indeed the lesson the next day could go in one of several directions, depending on what the students produce.

Application

Task

A new topic is introduced part-way through a lesson, for example polygons. Ask students to discuss what they know about names and properties of polygons and then write all these 'facts' on the board. Then ask the students to draw two separate circles using compasses. The homework is to think of ways to cut their circles (pies) into various numbers of equal pieces and to think about the question 'How can I be sure my circle is cut into equal pieces?'.

Comments

The pooled knowledge provides the starting point for new work; through this the teacher assesses what the students know and also provides everyone with a place to start thinking. The homework is open-ended and will generate the raw material for the next lesson. The task is posed as 'being sure'; thus it is about reasoning, rather than just doing what is asked. The circle drawing creates a link between topics, and the potential link is not obvious from this lesson. Rather than make this explicit, the teacher retains an element of surprise. In the next lesson, the sectored circles will be used to generate discussion about properties of regular polygons, but could equally well be used to remind students that fractions have to be equal parts.

Further reading

Ahmed, A. (Low Attainers in Mathematics Project) (1987) *Better Mathematics*, London: HMSO

Askew, M., Brown, M., Rhodes, V., Johnson, D. & Wiliam, D. (1997) *Effective teachers of numeracy*, London: King's College

Black, P., Harrison, C., Lee, C., Marshall, B. & Wiliam, D. (2002) *Working inside the black box: assessment for learning in the classroom*, London King's College

Boaler, J. (1997) *Experiencing School Mathematics*, Buckingham: Open University Press

Cuoco, A., Goldenberg, E.P. & Mark, J. (1996) 'Habits of Mind: an organizing principle for mathematics curricula', *Journal of Mathematical Behavior*, 15, 375–402

De Geest, E., Watson, A. & Prestage, S. (2003) 'Thinking in ordinary lessons: what happened when nine teachers believed their failing students could think mathematically' in B. Dougherty, N. Pateman & J. Zilliox (eds) *Proceedings of the 27th annual conference of the International Group for the Psychology of Mathematics Education*, 2, 301–308

Denvir, B. & Brown, M. (1986) 'Understanding of number concepts in low attaining 7–9 year olds: Parts I and II', *Educational Studies in Mathematics*, 17, 15–36 and 143–164

Dweck, C.S. (1999) *Self-theories: Their role in motivation, personality and development*, Philadelphia: Psychology Press

Hiebert, J., Gallimore, R., Garnier, H., Givvin, K.B., Hollingsworth, H., Jacobs, J., Chiu, A.M.Y., Wearne, D., Smith, M., Kersting, N., Manaster, A., Tseng, E., Etterbeek, W., Manaster, C., Gonzales, P. and Stigler, J. (2003) *Teaching Mathematics in Seven Countries: Results From the TIMSS 1999 Video Study (NCES 2003–013)*. U.S. Department of Education. Washington, DC: National Center for Education Statistics

Mason, J., Burton L. & Stacey, K. (1982) *Thinking Mathematically*, London: Addison Wesley

Ollerton, M. (2002) *Learning and teaching mathematics without a textbook*, Derby: Association of Teachers of Mathematics

Ollerton, M. and Watson, A. (2001) *Inclusive Mathematics 11–18*, London: Continuum

Perks, P. & Prestage, S. (2001) 'Doing mathematics with one TV and a spreadsheet', Cobden, D. (ed) *More Teaching, Learning and Mathematics with I.C.T.*, Derby: Association of Teachers of Mathematics

Prestage, S. and Perks, P. (2001) *Adapting and extending secondary mathematics activities: new tasks for old*, London: David Fulton

Prestage, S. & Perks, P. (2005) 'Generalising arithmetic: an alternative to algebra (or things to do with a plastic bag)', Watson, A., Houssart, J. & Roaf, C. (eds) *Supporting Mathematical Thinking*, London: David Fulton in association with NASEN, 106–118

Skemp, R.R. (1976) 'Relational understanding and instrumental understanding', *Mathematics Teaching*, 77, 20–26

Watson, A., De Geest, E. & Prestage, S. (2003) *Deep Progress in Mathematics: the Improving Attainment in Mathematics Project.* http://www.atm.org.uk/reviews/books/deepprogressinmathematics.html

Watson, A. & Mason, J. (1998) *Questions and Prompts for Mathematical Thinking*, Derby: Association of Teachers of Mathematics